TIPS, TECHNIQUES, INSPIRATIONAL RAMBLINGS, CREATIVE NUDGINGS AND STEP-BY-STEP INSTRUCTIONS TO HELP YOU CREATE

dragons

CHRISTI FRIESEN

Ok, here's the dealio with this book. But first, a flashback moment.

I've been the arty type forever. When I was growing up, my siblings and I had a lot of art and craft supplies at our fingertips and a kiln was one of them. My dad played around with throwing pots and we kids played around with clay. (I was never good at pots). So, around eight or nine, I had one of those defining moments. I can vividly remember sitting down eager to make something great. I had the desire, the energy, the supplies, the time -- but I had no ideas. Nothing. Two hours of mushing clay into weird little shapes and getting frustrated. I know I had had some really terrific, fantastic ideas earlier, but what were they? I sadly put the clay away for the day and drowned my sorrows in grape juice.

From that day on I kept notebooks and I sketched out ideas when I had them so that I'd have plenty to choose from when I needed them, which brings me to the point of this story and the point of this book. If you've picked up this book, you probably have anything from a passing interest to a life-altering addiction when it comes to creating things. (I'm in the second group.) So, this series of books, called "Beyond Projects", is intended to help with those times when you just want to make something and need a little idea nudge. The step-by-step layout should be helpful to your creative process by providing a sense of where you're going and how you'll end up. That in itself is satisfying, I think. But I also want to help inspire you to move beyond a mere project that starts and ends the same every time.

So, you'll find exact steps and techniques to make one dragon. But you'll also find lots of ideas, suggestions, tips, ramblings, and creative nudgings to help you discover your inner dragons and help them see the light of day.

There may also be a few jokes.

cf

Why dragons?

Oh, you know why. They're interesting. They can be magical, spiritual, regal, frightening, cute. Plus, since they're nonexistent, no one can say if you've made one correctly, which is always a nice bonus to creativity.

A few common elements we can all agree on -- long tail (most of the time), a serpentine body (or not), pointy-ish teeth (possibly), wings (sometimes.) After that, it's all up to your imagination.

In this book we'll sculpt a dragon focal bead using polymer clay embellished with beads and pearls.

First, a word or two about polymer clay:

I am not going to attempt to redo what has been done superbly by many others, namely, give you the basics about polymer clay conditioning, storage, baking, and care. There are a number of great books already that do this better than I could. If you are unfamiliar with polymer clay, flip to the resource pages in the back of this book, and familiarize yourself with a couple of clay basics. I'll wait for you to get back.

Hmmm mm hmmmm hmm mmmmm.

See, it's easy. Not too much stuff to worry about.

Now a very few specifics. There are several brands of polymer clay to choose from. Different brands have different characteristics and specialties. For this book, I will be using and recommending Premo! (a Sculpey product) which is a wonderful clay for sculpting (not too firm and not too soft), and it is very durable after it's been baked.

A word or two about embellishments:

glass beads, semi-precious stone beads, gems

For the embellishments of our dragon, we will use stones and beads and pearls wired into the clay while it is uncured. This way, they become a part of the design with clay details encircling and enfolding them.

Of course, this means they will be baked in the oven along with the clay. So, all beads and embellishments that can stand up to an hour in a 275° oven are groovy. This means all natural pearls, any stone (gemstone, semi-precious, even gravel from your driveway), and glass, crystal and some resins. If you're not sure, you may want to experiment with a sample piece first and put it in the oven at 275° for 20-30 minutes and see if it survives. Better the beginnings of a meltdown on a piece of foil than in the center of a dragon masterpiece.

pearls

Embellishments to avoid using:

wood • bamboo • most plastics or mystery rhinestones-that-might-be plastic-who-knows?
• seeds and plant materials
• chocolate (but this is a recomended tool for enhancing creativity)
• amber is a maybe (some ambers hold their color, but most darken too much in the oven)

fossils, shells, rocks, crystals

you will need these things

thick wire/rod for armatures
and holding open stringing holes

pasta machine, not
necessary, but very useful

acrylic paint, brushes
and sponges

beads for embellishments

varnish/clear coating -- many
good brands available

oven/baking pan,
oven thermometer

metal craft wire -- 28gauge
wire cutters and
chain-nose pliers

wooden sculpting tools,
needle-nose tweezers,
blade cutter/craft knife,
needle tool, and any
other groovy tool you
might have

and polymer clay,
of course!

One of the things that has made me a huge fan of polymer clay as an art medium is that it's colored and has such wonderful blending capabilities. Excuse me while I wax eloquent about this for a moment.

Because of the colors, you can mix and blend and create patterns that are used as your piece progresses. You don't have to imagine the final result, like you would if the clay still needed to be glazed or painted. I find this irresistible!

When I start a project, I choose my basic colors and then mix the clays so that I get blends and stripes and variations. It's like having a palette of options ready to choose from. Obviously here is where your pasta maker is your best tool. Pick dots or rolls or bits of color and blend them to achieve different stripes and swirls. Roll the clay mix through the pasta machine on the widest setting and check each pass before running through again. I try to look for cool blends, which I cut out and set aside, before re-running the wad through the machine again. When you're done, you should have several bits and slices of interesting blends in addition to your main color. These will come in very handy for accents later.

okay, already! let's sculpt

→ this guy!

Wendeyll

1. clay time

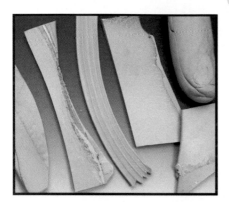

The colors for Wendeyll are a mix of Premo! colors -- ecru, gold, and green pearl. Mix a base color (for the body and wings), and some variations and blends to have as choices for details. This is your choice as to proportions of color to mix -- depends on whether you like your dragon more green, more golden or more creamy!

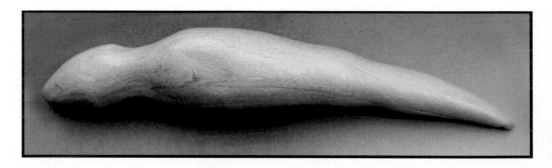

2. nice body

This is the most abstract and intuitive of all the steps, so of course it's right at the beginning (might as well get the hardest part done right away, huh?)

To make the body shape, you will want to gently manipulate the clay into a lump for a head, squeeze to a neck, fat again for a lump of a body and a long tapering tail, ending in a point. Simple, huh? What you are trying for is a gently undulating shape that hints at the dragon to come.

One reason that I suggest doing it this way, (instead of making a ball for a head and sticking it on a larger ball for a body and adding a tail) is that the finished dragon will have a much more realistic feel this way -- all one sinuous flow. You want to make your dragon look like he's alive and just curled up resting a bit before he uncoils and flies away.

So, start with a lump of your base color (about the size of a walnut) and roll it into a fat log, then start working it with your fingers (or someone else's fingers if you like, although I find that much harder to do). Squeeze gently at the snout end to make it more pointy, pinch gently for the neck, squeeze and pull for the tail. You want to do the tail last so that if you have too much clay, you can pinch away the excess from that end.

smooth   pinch   taper   snip

tip: I like using a piece of card stock paper as my work surface, so that my clay doesn't get stuck to the table. Then the card stock can go right into the oven for baking.

another tip:
Polymer clay picks up your warmth and the warmth of your environment, causing it to soften and get more sticky, droopy or stretchy. You can minimize that by washing your hands in cool water (and get the clay residue off too, which cuts down on the stickiness), or putting the clays you are using in the fridge for a bit to cool down. Or you can wait until winter.

dragon profile
Wendeyll

This is Wendeyll, he'll be your dragon for this book. Wendeyll is a quiet, thoughtful little guy, with a special fondness for cheese. Especially Swiss cheese, as he enjoys crawling into one of the little holes and eating his way into the interior. It's like a little fort in there.

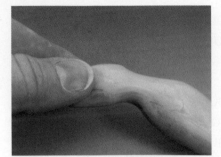

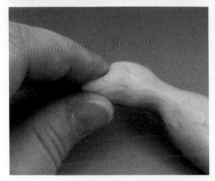

3. heads up

The head is a very simple shape. Finish the pinching and molding you started until you have a shape you like. If the snout gets too long, just pinch or cut some away and keep manipulating.

To make the indentations that will serve as eye sockets, just grip the face in your thumb and forefinger and squeeze (not too much, it's not toothpaste -- that's not enough, you didn't even make a dent, yeah -- that's perfect!) You'll probably need to flatten the top of his head down a bit after all that squooshing.

Experiment with different face shapes. Wendeyll's here is only one of many options. (As you make more dragons, keep experimenting -- just small adjustments can make a lot of difference in the finished look!)

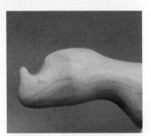

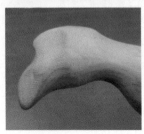

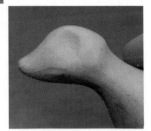

tip: Don't let the body and tail get too bent out of shape while you're focused on the head. Work close to your table to keep gravity from elongating the neck and creating a giraffe-dragon.)

All of the lineup of heads on the right are essentially the same shape, with minor variations -- see what a difference a lil' bit of tweakin' can do for their personalities?

Who you calling "big nose" Big Nose?

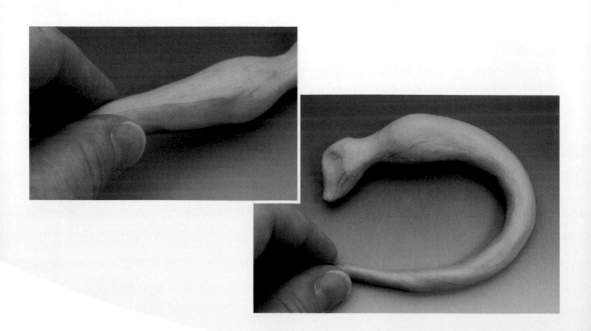

4. the tail curl

Once you have the basic face shape
done, finish elongating and smoothing the tail and rolling it into a snail-like coil.

Obviously, there are a bunch of different ways to make a dragon's tail and I fully expect you'll want to experiment with that, but here I suggest this simple coil tail for several reasons. First, it's easy, so it's good to learn on. Second, it can be changed very simply which allows for a lot of individual creativity. Third, if you do it right, you can get away with no dragon hands and feet and nobody misses them, which keeps this project easy for all skill levels to accomplish! Oh yeah, and fourth, it looks cool, don't you think?

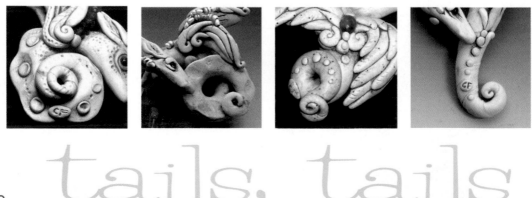

tails, tails

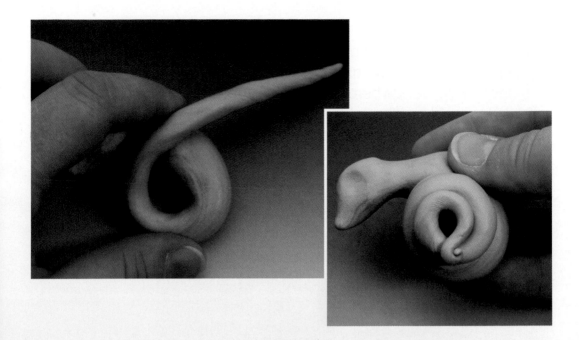

Start by bending the body (not the tail yet) --
again for realism. If you were a curled up dragon, your
back would bend, not just your tail, right? Keep bending and
then curl the tail around and around until you run out of tail. (I ended
Wendeyll's tip in a little backwards flip just for fun). I always try to make
the tail curl up and over where the arm and leg would have been
attached, making their absence unnoticed. Also, gently but firmly press
the tail clay into the body and into the coils, but without mashing, as you
go along. Polymer clay has a wonderful ability to stick to itself for a
strong connection, but needs to be firmly pressed together to do so.

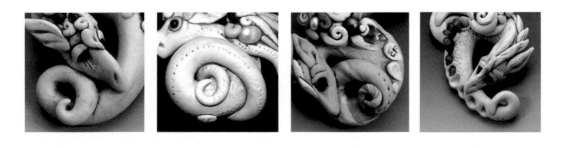

& more tails

5. pinch wing pads

With that same ol' thumb and forefinger trick, pinch the area at the base of the neck where the shoulder would be, like you did the eye socket. This will make a pad where the wings can be attatched.

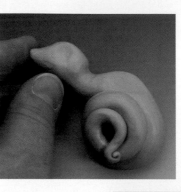

6. head tilt

Before you add any details, it's a good idea to get the face angle right. Play with a couple of options. Is he looking up at you? Behind his back at an approaching gryphon? Tucked down into his tail coils for a little nap?

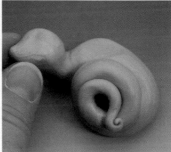

For Wendeyll, I chose a very simple "head-down, thinking about delicious cheese, mmmmm" look.

7. just winging it

The wings are very simple shapes that are made more dramatic by adding lots of details on top.

Start by making a two balls of clay. Roll each ball into teardrop or cone shapes and flatten with your fingers, bending them into curves slightly as you flatten.

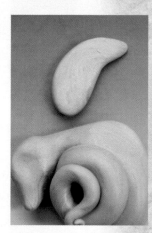

tip: When you're making two matching things like wings or ears or sofas, it's a good idea to make both of the clay balls that you'll use at the same time so that they are symmetrical.

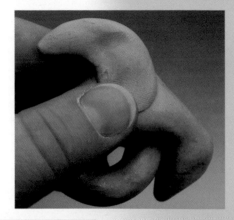

Now, flatten the fat end of one wing a little more and attach by pressing it firmly to the back of the dragon's "wing pad". Make sure it's firmly attached (but don't smoosh the rest of your dragon while you're attaching!)

In order to keep a hole open for stringing your bead later, lay a piece of wire (at least 16 gauge or thicker), or a skewer, dowel or similar straight rod down on top of the wing shape where it meets the body. This will be removed after baking.

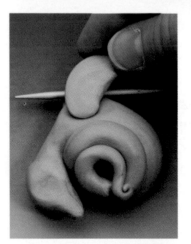

Position the top wing over the bottom wing and press down firmly. I often like to make the underneath wing show a little, instead of them being exactly on top of each other so that there is the feeling of depth. Press the two wings together, around the wire/rod.

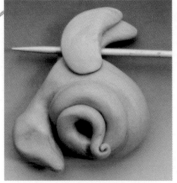

Now is the time to see how the bead will hang and adjust the position of the wings or head if necessary to get the look you want. Carefully hold the "so-far" dragon up using the wire/rod in the wings to see how your dragon will hang when he's part of a necklace. Push the wings and head around carefully to adjust until you're happy.

8. the eyes have it

Let the wings and all of the fun accents we're going to add later just simmer in your imagination while we go back to the dragon's facial features!

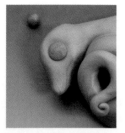

Doing the eyes as the first detail will establish the attitude of your dragon and that sometimes dictates what other features you will add to the wings and body. Sometimes you are thinking of one expression, and your dragon will fool you and come up with his own attitude -- I find it best not to argue with a dragon, just let him have his way in this.

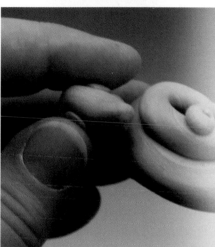

First, make two little balls of clay (about the size of BBs) out of some of the clay " variations" that you set aside when you were mixing colors and blends (I suggest a contrasting color).
In Wendeyll's case I used gold clay.

Place the balls in the middle of the socket area and press firmly, flattening them. I like to flatten both of them at the same time so I can use the pressure to push against each other, that way I don't squash any other part of the head.

Some eye-opening facts that I just now made up:

The eyes are the most important aspect of a sculpture if you want it to have some personality. The eyes are the mirrors of the soul, and all that stuff.

Dark beads make the best eyes.

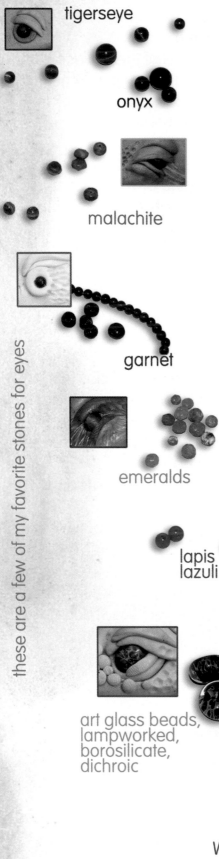

tigerseye

onyx

malachite

garnet

emeralds

lapis
lazuli

these are a few of my favorite stones for eyes

art glass beads,
lampworked,
borosilicate,
dichroic

9. wiring the eye beads

Yes, Wendeyll has beady little eyes, literally. His eyes are tigerseye beads.

Wiring the beads is a simple technique and one that I recommend you use on every bead you add to your sculptures. Oh, you could just press the bead in and hope for the best, I suppose -- but that is really just expecting that a piece of stone or glass will stick into plastic, and there's a pretty good chance that won't be long-lasting. I like to wire in every bead because a piece of twisted wire embedded into the clay does help to keep the bead tucked in, and if the bead does pull out (which it sometimes does), then the hole made by the wire is an excellent place for a dab of glue to really anchor.

glass seed beads

zombie

not zombie

Whatever bead you pick for the eye, it should be darker than the clay. if the eye is too light, you get a zombie dragon

To wire the eye beads (and all other single bead embellishments that you will be doing), snip an inch or so of metal craft wire (I recommend 28 gauge) and thread it through the bead's hole. Grip the wire and bend it so that the wires bend back parallel to each other and the bead is centered between the wires. Grip the wire in your pliers and twirl the bead with your fingers so that the wire twists firmly up to the base of the bead. Don't overdo it, or the wire will snap, don't underdo it or the wire will be loose (which is harder to work with). With wire cutters, snip off all but a quarter-inch tail of twisted wire.

Now you're ready to stab the beaded wire wherever it is needed. In this case, into the flattened ball of clay in the eye socket area (this all sounds a little more icky than it should, huh?) Again, since Wendeyll here has eyes on both sides of his head, press the eyes in at the same time, using the force of pushing against each other to prevent squishing anywhere else. Incidentally, I don't always go to the trouble of making a full face with features on both sides. Since a finished focal bead is worn with one side against the body, there is no reason to make the back side of the face unless it will be visible, or unless you feel like it. I just felt like it - you can do whichever you like (I won't tell if you only do one side, I promise.)

Press the eye bead into the clay until the bead is embedded, usually so that the bead hole where the wire comes out is just covered, if possible. This is especially important on the eyes (unless you like that crazy googly-eyed look.)

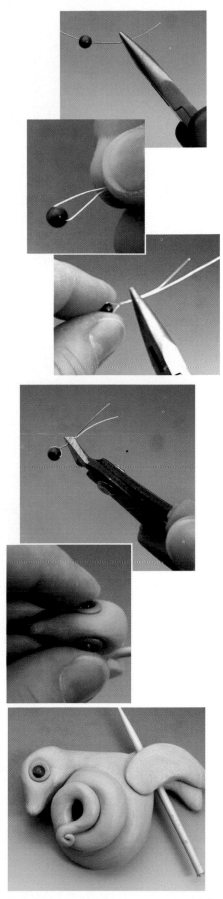

10. it's just an expression

Ok, now the eye beads are in. Your dragon probably has a surprised, or wide-awake look right now, huh? I like that look and often leave it at that, but if you want to do eyelids and brows, here's how (and why).

Eyelids are a primary way to convey expression with your sculpture. You can make them as simple or detailed as you wish by adding multiple eyelids and playing with the texture and detailing around the eyes also.

These eyelids are simply little rice-shaped pieces of clay that are curved and flattened above the eye bead. I like to use the contrast colors here and often end with the last lid in the row (if I'm doing multiples) being the same color as the dragon's body so that it blends smoothly into the head. There!

We'll save some final texture and small details around the eyes until the very last, so they won't get smudged by other sculpting details.

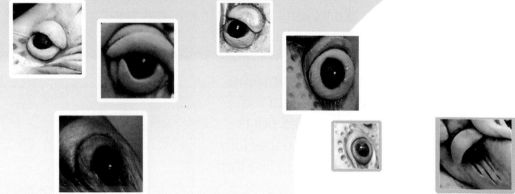

11. **pick your nose**

Well, you already picked your dragon's nose shape, but I just couldn't resist that topic heading. Sometimes nostrils seem appropriate to me, sometimes not. Did you hear about the dragon with no nostrils? How did he smell? Just as bad as ever.

Sorry.

There are a few ways to make nostrils (just look below).

For Wendeyll, just a simple poke in the snout with a pointy thing will do.

poked hole nostril

dot of clay, then poked hole nostril

big ol' honker nostril -- & I have to open my mouth because my allergies are acting up and I can't breathe

expressions

yarg!

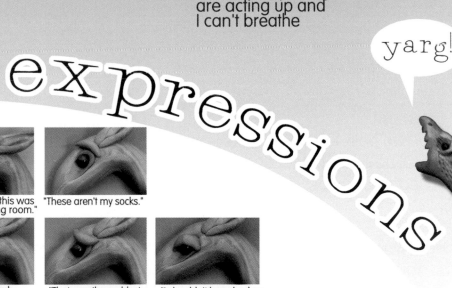

"Oops. I thought this was the men's dressing room."

"These aren't my socks."

"Give me back my sandwich."

"That was the saddest movie I've ever seen."

"I shouldn't have had so much allergy medication."

"Huh?"

"I REALLY shouldn't have had so much allergy medication."

"Sooo sleeepy..."

"I'm outta here!"

21

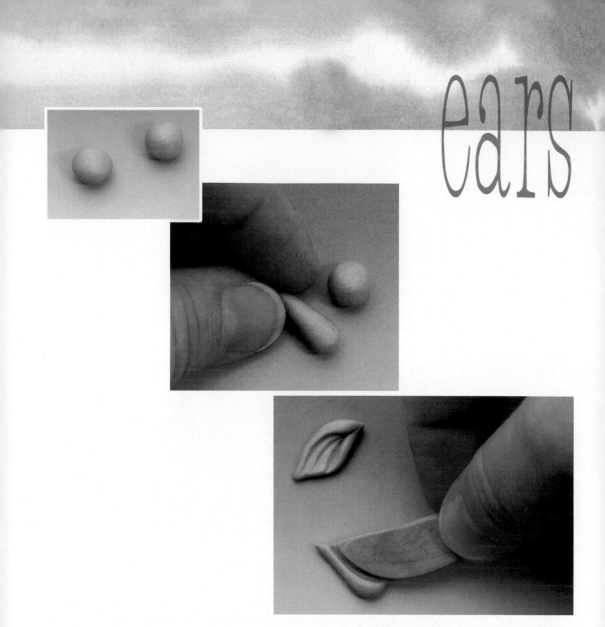

12. listen up!

Roll out two balls for the ears, like you did for the eye socket balls, only these will be a little bigger and the same color as the body. Roll them into a teardrop shape, like you did for the wings, and flatten them slightly.

Using a wooden sculpting tool, you can press several creases into the ears. You don't have to though, they can look good without that, too. Pick the ear up and pinch the rounded end to create a cup-like fold. See, doesn't that make them look more ear-y! You can use your blade to slice off some of the thickness on the back so that it lays flatter on the head if you like.

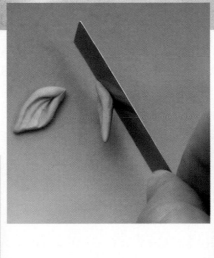

Press the ears into the side of the head a bit behind the eyes, but not too far down the neck. Tweak 'em to make them look the way you want: perky, shy, hang-dog. I might suggest that you keep them laying down onto the neck or touching together on top of the head, or some similar arrangement, to add some strength and stability. Since your bead is going to be worn, things that stick out are subject to more stress and possible breakage, so be mindful of that when you choose your final ear placement. Of course, if you're going to hang this one on the wall, do whatever you like with the ears!

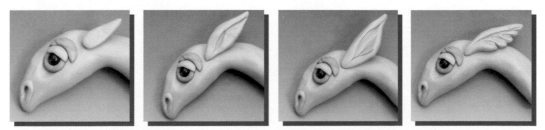

for an additional fee, you can upgrade your dragon to any of these fine options

13. I love your accent

It's time for my favorite part, which I hope you will find just as fun. The "hard" part is over -- making the dragon look like a dragon. Now it's time for the accents and embellishments. These will be a mixture of clay and beads, and the best way is to work them in together. A bead becomes a focal point around which clay is worked which then inspires more beaded accents. You see what I'm getting at here.

Let's start with a larger stone (or in Wendeyll's case, a green pearl) as the launching point for wing accents. The pearl is wired in the same way as the eye beads were. Jam it straight in and embed it into the clay a bit, just like before.

Now is the time you get to use the best of your clay blends where they will really shine! Cut the nicest bits into thin strips and roll gently or manipulate into snakes and coils.

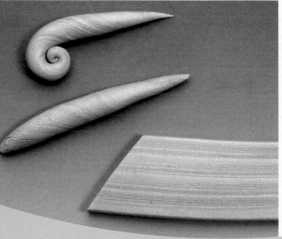

Work around the large pearl and add other pearls, stones or beads as you are inspired. You can have the clay overlap the bead as long as it is still firmly attached to other clay somewhere. Remember that ol' "clay not sticking well to glass and stone" concept we chatted about earlier -- it still applies, so make sure your clay accents are well grounded, so to speak. Keep on adding accents -- clay, bead, clay, bead, clay, bead....

don't
mind
me, just
passin'
thru

For the embellishments on the head, why not echo what you're doing on the wings. For Wendeyll, I again started with a pearl and worked curls and snakes of clay over it, like the wings, and topped it off with more pearls. Wendeyll has a thing for pearls.

Little clay dots can be a fun accent -- balls of clay pressed into the body of your dragon. I followed the curve of the spine which you'll notice echos the circular theme started with the pearls (wasn't that kinda' clever?) You can press a wired bead or pearl into some or all of the dots, too -- that can look pretty neat. Okay, let's let Wendeyll rest while we follow that guy -->

Want more embellishment
and accent ideas?

Follow me

Meet some of my friends. I think you'll get some good ideas about accents and flourishes and coloring and details that you can use on your projects.

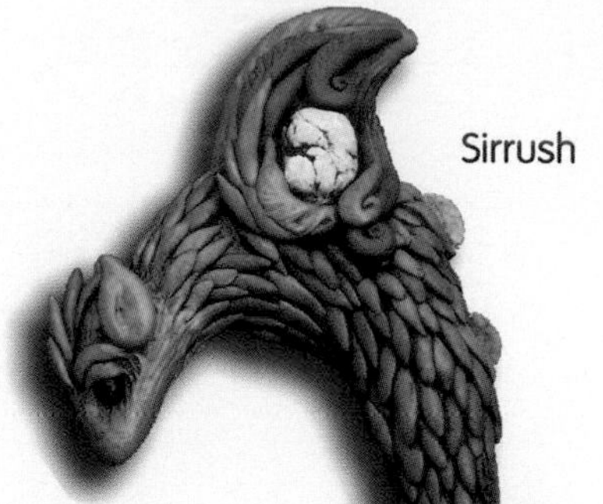

Sirrush

Little Boy Blue

Tip: When doing spread wings, the wire/rod for the stringing hole goes horizontally thru the body, under the wings

Woodrid

Koral Belle

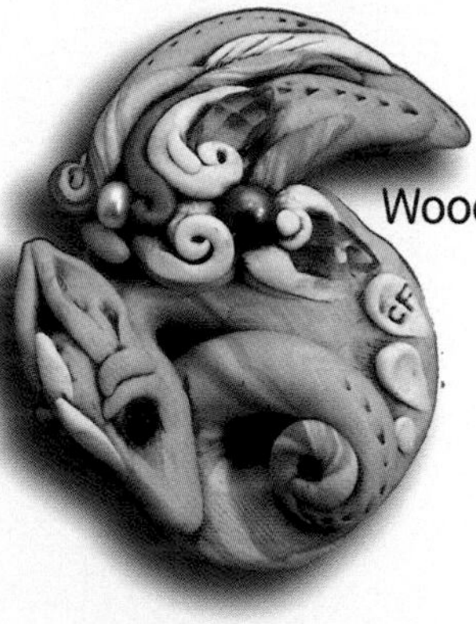

Thistle

Flit

Fawna

28

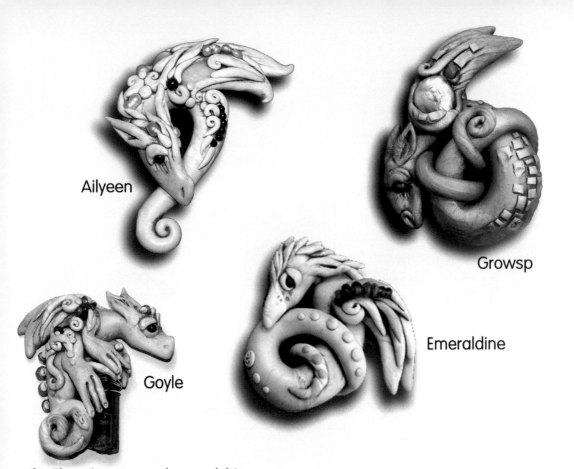

Ailyeen

Growsp

Goyle

Emeraldine

tip: The wire wrapped around this tourmaline crystal is twisted and embedded into the clay between the legs/arms for a more firm attachment.

dragon profile

OLD YELLER

HEY! I'M NOT SO OLD!
I'M ONLY 213! I CAN STILL
BEAT YOU UP! OH YEAH?!
COME OVER HERE AND SAY THAT!
HEY! WHERE ARE YOU GOING?!
CAN'T YOU TAKE A JOKE?!

I'll be good.

Boulder opal cabochon and accent beads of pearl and garnet.

Faceted garnet

This garnet bead has a little crown made from a sterling silver spacer.

A focal stone can be the anchor point for curls and swirls of clay.

round lapis bead.

Coil a bit of goldfilled wire like a snail's curl (don't forget to bend the straight end back into a staple for a firm grip) then impale a square bead into a dragons back for an unusual ridge design

I'm hungry.

Dots pressed into the clay make a nice bumpy texture.

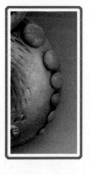

Embed a stone bead, then use a ball of clay to cover the wire, giving a very natural feel to the stone embellishment.

Here's a swell pattern -- curls and swirls and dots.

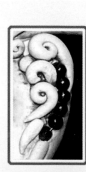

String a row of beads on a single wire for this look.

These feathers start with a snail coil and curve.

Tuck in beads between the feathers.

Feathery wings are made with flattened tapers of clay (rice shapes or leaf shapes).
Carve in the central line and radiating strokes with a needle tool. The patina will bring out the details.

This is just a funky wing. Do with it whatever you will.

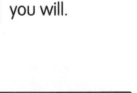

All of these wings feature a snail curl around which all the other embellishments flow.

This wing started out in the same flattened leaf shape and details were added with sculpture tool and needle tool resulting in a more batlike look. Kinda.

31

lapis

citrine

emerald

carnelian

A lineup of beads on a single strand of wire really accentuate the curve of a design -- they look especially good in wings.

Little dots of clay are fun and can be squished onto your dragon's body to make a great pattern. You can stick things in the little dots -- like beads of course, but also shells, crystals, and other stuff you may have lying around.

More single bead accents and the clay embellishments worked around them.

Mosaics make a great pattern, especially along the ridge of a tail or the center of a body. To make mosaic squares, flatten clay quite thin and slice with a very sharp blade. Position squares with the tip of the blade.

This guy has furry bits and dotty bits and strands of turquoise chips as a kind of mane.

Use a needle tool or other pointed tool to scratch or poke little hair lines. The patina will grab these grooves and add depth.

Poke some dimples with a pointy tool.

Little rice-shaped bits of clay make fabulous furry texture.

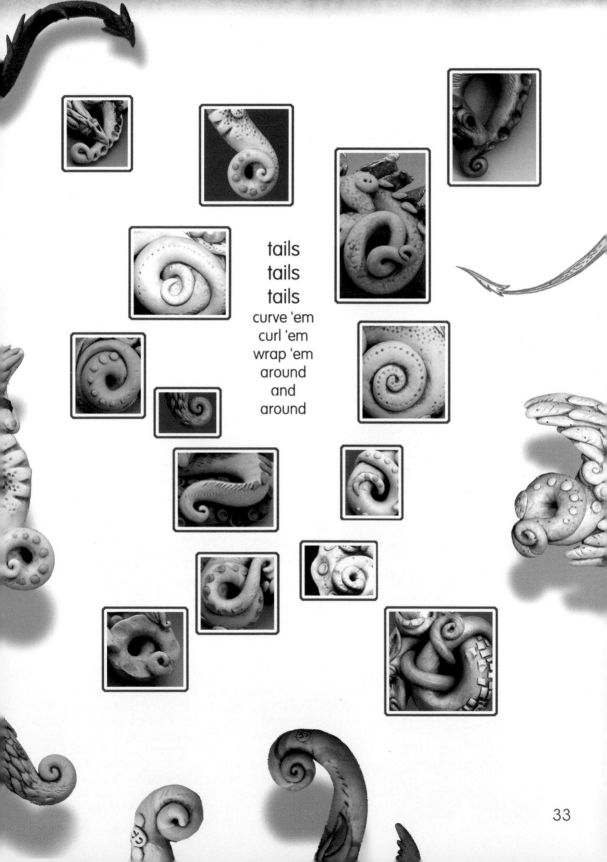

**tails
tails
tails**
curve 'em
curl 'em
wrap 'em
around
and
around

And now back to our regularly scheduled programing.

14. texture

Once you've added as many beaded and clay accents as you want, the final touch is adding texture to your dragon. Could be a lot, could be a little, could be none. Wendeyll here is being a sport and letting me do almost every single sculpture trick to him for the purposes of your edification, so he'll get all textured out too. Experiment on a piece of clay you're not using at the moment and see what kind of texture you can create using all kinds of things. (See the next page for some ideas.)

I've used a very simple texture technique -- poking the clay with a pointy tool to make lots of little dotty dimples (as you can see, I'm still echoing that circular theme). The great thing about texture is that it is a great place for color to get trapped when we get to the patina step.

I've also done a couple of other little finishing touches here that you may want to play with. Like pressing in lines in the part of the exposed back wing and spreading out the "pancake" from under the eye bead with little lines in front. And I also added a bit of gold clay to the ear and dimpled it with the pokey tool. Just the last little touches.

DRAGON PROFILE

I'm Flit. It's who I am and what I do. The dragonflies are all jealous cuz they aren't jeweled like me with my pearls and magical peridot. And that's real gold in my wings. Fairy gold. It didn't come cheap, though. I can tell you. I traded with the Fairy Queen Mother and now every full moon eve I have to let her brood of grandchildren ride around all night on my back and their hands are always sticky and that redheaded one pinches. Ah well, what price glory.

texture tips

this pointy sculpture tool
makes fun scales

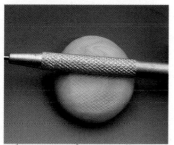

the grip of a needle tool
makes this pattern which
the patina will highlight

this is one of those sticks
you find with weird insect trails

this is a wormhole-riddled
shell I found -- neat, huh?

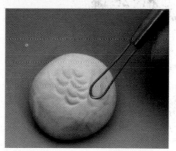

another clay sculpture tool
that makes wonderful scales

this tool is a knitting needle
with a glass bead superglued
on the tip

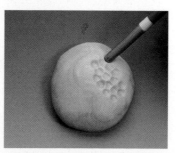

dimples courtesy of the
rounded end of a paintbrush

35

15. and how would you like your dragon cooked?

Follow the clay manufacturer's directions, which should mean baking your dragon for at least 30 - 45 minutes at 275° in a dependable oven. Cooking is a very important part of the durability of a finished polymer clay piece. Too cool a temperature, or not long enough in the oven and the final piece will be more likely to be brittle. Too long or two hot and polymer clay will burn and the fumes can be harmful.

Basically, a home oven or larger convection oven works the best. Toaster ovens have to be watched diligently because they have this volcano-like tendency to spike in temperature for some reason. Get a oven thermometer and pull up a chair and a good book and keep an eye on things if you're unfamiliar with your oven's tendencies.

You can minimize polymer clay residue in your oven by covering the pan with foil. (Polymer clay releases fumes when baked which condense inside the oven to re-permeate the next thing to be baked -- which if it's Aunt Malinda's famous lemon meringue up-side-down brownies, could cause trouble, if you see what I mean.) Many people designate an oven specifically to polymer clay so they don't have to keep cleaning out the clay residue every time they want to bake those famous brownies.

Baking is not difficult, but is important. Just remember: temperature and time. Get those two squared away and you're set.

16. cooling

Well, this one's obvious. Take your dragon out and let him cool. Remember to keep ventilation going to take away any lingering polymer clay fumes. Polymer hardens as it cools, so it's going to seem soft and not finished cooking yet. Don't worry, it'll be fine.

17. pull the wire

When your dragon is cool enough to handle you can use pliers to twist and gently pull out the metal wire between the wings that was used to keep the stringing hole open.

twist
pull
twist
pull
yank

ah, that's much better

DRAGON PROFILE

SIRRUSH

I AM SIRRUSH. I HAVE SEEN THE RISE AND FALL OF EMPIRES, THE GRANDEUR AND FOLLY OF MONARCHS. MY NAMESAKE GUARDED THE ENTRY INTO GREAT BABYLON. HE SLUMBERS NOW, HIS DUTIES FORGOTTEN, BUT I REMAIN. THEY DIDN'T TELL ME WHERE ELSE TO GO. MAYBE I'LL GO CHECK OUT NEW YORK CITY.

18. patina

This is an optional step. If you like your dragon just the way he is, skip this and move on to the next part! Otherwise, now is the time for all those cracks and crevices and dimples and texture to do their thing -- trap paint and add a depth and richness to the piece.

Use acrylic paint for this and make sure your dragon is completely cooled down first. If he's still warm, the paint will dry super fast and make it difficult to rub off. Any brand is good (I use Liquitex personally) and any color works -- depends on your preference. I tend to use a lot of browns because I like that antique-y look -- like the piece is an artifact from some ancient palace or something. Delusions of grandeur, I know.

Mix your paint (I used a combo of burnt umber, raw sienna and burnt sienna for Wendeyll) and brush on with a dry (or very slightly damp) brush. Water added to the paint or brush tends to cause the paint to bead off the clay, which is no fun. Make sure you jam the paint down deep into the cracks and crevises. This is where the paint will stay, so get it down in there. Now, with a very rung out sponge (again, wet is bad), wipe off the paint from the surface, leaving it only in the cracks. The more you wipe, the more paint will come off and only the deepest creases will stay patina-ed, so adjust according to your taste.

You will need several sponges and you will have to constantly rinse them out and wring them dry. If you try to keep using a sponge saturated with paint, all you will do is smear paint all over your dragon and he'll just look muddy and sad. So brush on, rub off and rinse and wring and repeat. If you have any pockets that resist the sponge and are collecting too much paint, you can use a clean paintbrush to plunge the clog out!

19. varnish

After the patina paint is dry, it's time to add a varnish. If you skipped the patina stage, it's still time to add a varnish. Of course, you can skip the varnishing entirely, in which case, just skip ahead to the next page.

Coating with a clear, protective coating is not necessary, but helps keep your patina from getting scratched, or if you skipped the patina, it helps protect your dragon bead from stains and either way, adds a nice finished look. There are several things you can use and a few you shouldn't -- again, go check out those authors wiser and more experienced than me in these things. I recommend Sculpey glaze (in stain or glossy) or Diamond Wood Finish Varathane by Flecto (it's a water based varnish that for some reason works great on polymer clay. You can get it at hardware stores.)

20. one more bake

Let your dragon dry. Again. Then the last trick is a pop back into the oven to set the paint and/or varnish. Just a little extra step to add durability. Lay your dragon on a fresh piece of cardstock and bake at 200° for about 15-20 minutes.

Now that Wendeyll is done, what should we do with him?

Obviously, a necklace focal piece is the most logical, since he is a focal bead. Won't he attract attention all snuggled in your neck like that?!

If you'd rather he adorn a wall or other decorative nook, you can make a hanging out of him by stringing him with a piece of leather cording, ribbon or beaded loop. Now he's ready to hang up for everyone to admire.

Of course, he can just curl up in a handfull of moss and make a great little sculpture.

arms & legs

Ok, so we've done a simple dragon with curled up tail which lets us get away with no arms or legs -- and get away with it pretty well, don't you think? The other dragons we've met so far show lots of variations on that limb-less theme. But what if you're feeling adventurous and generous and want to give your next dragon some appendages?

It's not hard, and all the steps are the same, except that you should leave the tail uncurled (or untwirled, unlooped or unwiggled) until after you have added the limbs.

Hands or legs are essentially the same, the legs are just a little bigger than the arms and have slightly longer toes.

Start with a log of clay. Slice two or three slits (depending on whether you want three or four fingers). Spread the pieces apart a bit and use your fingers to shape. You will want to very gently pinch to eliminate the cut edge and then round the fingers -- too much pressure and they will get stretched out of shape. If they do get too long, slice a little off the tip and re-smooth. A dowel or needle tool works nicely to smooth the gap between the fingers.

arm

Once your fingers (or toes) are to your liking, shape the arm or leg by gentle pinching and positioning. Cut off any excess to adjust the length of the finished limb.

leg

Hands should taper slightly at the wrist and can have an elbow bend.
Legs make a fairly sharp angle at the ankle and curve at the knee.

Attach firmly to your dragon and then position the tail.

If you are going to have him hold a stone or crystal, you will need both hands for grasping and you will want to make sure that the stone is firmly encased in fingers and maybe even cushioned by the tail or feet. Since the crystal probably can't be wired in, after he's baked, super glue will anchor the stone if it is loose.

Okay, now what else can we do with dragons?

cabochon

A cabochon, or cab, is a domed piece, usually round or oval, with a flattened base. You can make one with a dragon on top.

To make a cabochon, start with a ball of clay, and flatten on one side. Make your dragon as you would if he were a bead (but probably a bit smaller!) You will want to make the body shape and press it into the clay cab before adding the features and detail (less mushing than if you sculpted it completely and then tried to press it onto the base). Add details, and bake. Patina the same as for the focal bead.

Cabochons can be used in wire wrap projects, sewn into beaded projects, as brooches (see below) or whatever other project you can think of!

brooch

If you want to make a brooch, add a pin backing before the patina and varnishing stages. Use super glue to attach a hinged-back straight pin to the back side of the dragon. Hold for 15-30 seconds to set the glue.

Now, add a thin layer of liquid clay. Cover the back with a very thin layer of fresh clay, sandwiching the pin bar between your dragon and the fresh clay. The liquid clay will allow the clay to grab to the baked clay. You can cover the pin back with a simple square of clay, or with flattened balls of clay -- whichever is easier for you.

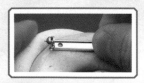

Make sure not to impede the moving parts of the pin with the new clay (although you can always trim away the problem clay after the piece is all finished baking if you need to).

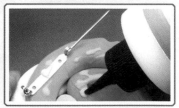

Bake again for at least 20-25 minutes and then complete with the patina and varnishing steps.

sculptures

With just a little tweaking, the same steps we used to make the dragon bead can be used to make dragon sculptures. These are a bit different than just putting your focal bead dragon in a bed of moss -- these dragons snuggle on their own base and have no stringing hole.

First make a round ball of clay and flatten it onto your card stock.

Next, make a dragon body shape in the same way as for the bead, but instead of rolling the tail up so that the piece all lays flat, roll or position the tail so that it hugs the base. Press the clay body into the clay base firmly but gently.

The wings are optional. If you do not add any, you can have more fun detailing the ridge of the back with embellishments. If you do add wings, first insert a small piece of thick wire (the same kind as we used to hold open the string hole in the focal bead steps). This will be used to provide support for the wings and will stay in the piece, so cover it completely by sandwiching it between the wing shapes.

All the other details are the same as for the focal bead.

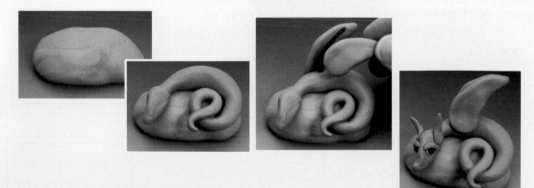

You can add some more accents to the base -- like grass (little ricey bits of clay) and stones (yellow and brown jade and turquoise work terrific) or flowers and berries (little coral rounds or garnets!)

For a larger sculpture, you can cover a rock with clay for the base and continue as usual. This will give the piece more weight so it can handle a larger dragon.

wire inside grass, for strength.

(this is liquid clay)

For more complicated dragon sculptures, armatures of wire and foil are used to build the shape first and then clay is used to cover the "skeleton" before details are added. It is really just a variation on what we've done so far, with a few more tricks and tips, but that is a subject for another book! Here are some examples just to whet your appetite and get your creative gears working!

My shells are spikes! I mean, my spikes are shells!

43

wall pieces & vessels

A wall piece is simply a piece that you hang on the wall. You know, art. It can be simple -- like your dragon strung on a cord and hung, or a larger, more elaborate scene.

To create a wall piece, first make a slab of clay for the sculpted dragon to lay on by running clay through the widest setting on your pasta machine until you have something you like as a background. You can press clay slabs together for larger pieces (don't make it bigger than your oven can handle, though!)

Sculpt your dragon onto the background, (as you would for a cabochon), and then add any decorative clay elements and beaded elements to complete your scene. Remember to leave holes or loops for the finished piece to be hung from. You can hang it directly through the holes, or make a beaded loop (or cord, or ribbon).

For a vessel, mix clay sheets as for the wall piece, run them through the pasta machine several notches thinner. Now cover any clean glass jar or vase with these clay sheets, completely encasing the outside and over the ridge into the inside. It's your choice as to how much of the interior you wish to cover.

Sculpt your dragon directly onto the clay-covered glass (the same way as for a cabochon). Since there is only a small layer of clay over the glass, it's trickier to add beaded accents to the covered vessel, but inserting the wire sideways, or through an added clay bit will usually do it! Bake as usual, the glass will take it!

Since your claywork is over glass, it will be able to hold water if you want to use it as a vase for a lovely spray of orchids or something. Just change the water daily and rinse and dry each time -- this isn't something you can just throw into the dishwasher, obviously! Of course, it's just great as an art piece all on it's own, I think. Don't you?